KOURTNEY KARDASHIAN

A SHORT UNAUTHORIZED BIOGRAPHY

FAMELIFE BIOS

1

WHO IS KOURTNEY KARDASHIAN

Kourtney Mary Kardashian is an American model, social media personality, and media figure. She and her siblings first mainly appeared on the tv program Keeping Up with the Kardashians in 2007. Because of its popularity, spin-offs such as Kourtney and Khloé Take Miami and Kourtney, and Kim Take New York were created. Kourtney seems to be in the wholesale and fashion industries with Kim and Khloé. They've marketed numerous clothing brands and beauty products, and the book Kardashian Konfidential, published in 2010. In early 2019, Kourtney started her blog, dubbed 'Poosh.'

Kourtney Mary Kardashian was born on April 18, 1979, in Los Angeles, California, to Robert and Kris Kardashian. Kim and Khloé are her younger siblings, and Rob is her brother. Her parents separated in 1991, and her mom tied the knot to Bruce Jenner, a decathlete who won the 1976 Summer Olympics. Jenner eventually switched her name to Caitlyn in 1991. Kardashian got stepbrothers Burton "Burt," Brandon, and Brody, as well as stepsister Casey and half-sisters Kendall and Kylie, due to their marriage.

Kardashian first gained popularity on television programs in 2005 with the show Filthy Rich: Cattle Drive, wherein she raised money for a good cause. Kim Kardashian, Superstar, a sex tape created by her sister Kim and former boyfriend Ray J in 2003, was unveiled in February 2007, mainly contributing to her rise to fame. Earlier that same year, Kardashian was cast in the reality tv show Keeping Up with the Kardashians alongside her mom Kris, stepfather Bruce, brother and sister Kim, Khloé, and Rob half-sisters Kendall and Kylie. The show was a massive success for E!, the station that broadcasts it, and it spawned numerous spin-offs, which include Kourtney and Khloé Take Miami, Khloé, and Lamar, and Kourtney and Kim Take New York. Kardashian and her mom launched Smooch, a kids clothing retailer in Los Angeles and New York City that carries the Crib Rock Couture brand. This program was a huge hit, and Kourtney Kardashian gained much attention and popularity. The American model made a starring appearance in the ABC soap opera "One Life to Live," portraying attorney Kassandra Kavanagh. The television star's second series, "Kourtney and Khloé Take the Hamptons," premiered in 2014.

Kourtney Kardashian is a successful business owner to become a model and a television show host. Kris and her mother launched the 'Smooch' clothing and accessories retailer. There are many clothing store locations in New York City and Los Angeles. Kourtney also co-owns and runs a clothing store called DASH. By her sisters, the American beauty started a fashion brand for the Bebe company in 2010. Kardashian and her sisters launched a sunless tanner named "Kardashian Glamour Tan" in that same year. Not only that! The Kardashian sisters have also started a jewelry line for the business Virgins, Angels, and Saints. Kourtney Kardashian is a spokesperson for the 'Quick Trim' body fat vitamin. She and her sisters also embody a skin care products business. Dr. Ron DiSalvo created this line, dubbed "perfect skin." The Kardashian siblings also wrote a book called 'Kardashian Konfidential,' published in 2010. Courtney Kardashian appeared in two parts of the sitcom "I Am Cait" in 2015. She even had a starring part in the film "Dash Dolls."

2

THINGS PEOPLE HAVE SAID ABOUT KOURTNEY KARDASHIAN

The Kardashians are not famous for their body-positive behaviors for the most part. They've been convicted of instilling a harmful fixation with trying to lose weight and looking gorgeous in the past. Supporters have noted that at least one Kardashian appears to have her priorities straight regarding physical aspects. Kourtney Kardashian is sending out big self-acceptance positive energy, and the media is loving it. Kardashian is well conscious of how her approach regarding her physique can ruin Penelope as a mother. That's why she chooses her words carefully. She warned her mum, Kris Jenner, not to use the word "fat" around Penelope in a KUWTK series. And Kardashian has witnessed firsthand how her demeanor affects her daughter. If her statements are any confirmation, she is exceptionally self-assured about her appearance. Kardashian recently shared a video on Instagram in which she answered questions from the public. According to one person, people were already commenting on her photos, wondering whether she was pregnant. Her reaction exemplified what it means to embrace yourself for who you are. 'That's how my body looks. I've put on a few more weights during my lockdown, but I love my body and am confident of my appearance. She highlighted that she isn't ashamed just to let others see how she appears to look, or she would not even be bringing herself over there in the first place. We're all different shapes, and that's my body, and I'm confident of it. And that's how I answer the negative criticism.

With all of the self-esteem issues that individuals encounter nowadays, it's encouraging seeing a woman accept her body, even if she has gained a little weight!" one fan said. Many people agree, describing her positive attitude as motivating. One fan exclaimed, "I adore her reaction, and I appreciate that she didn't photoshop out all the little portion of mama pudge she already has." Everyone can not help wondering if the Kardashians' empowering response wouldn't cause conflict. Whether or not Kardashian's body positivity sparks tension, it appears that many fans are relieved to see at least one member of the household maintaining a good attitude about their appearance.

KOURTNEY KARDASHIAN IS BORN

Kourtney Mary Kardashian was born on April 18, 1979, in Los Angeles, California, to Robert and Kris Kardashian. Kim and Khloé are her younger siblings, and Rob is her brother. Her parents separated in 1991, and her mom tied the knot to Bruce Jenner, a decathlete who won the 1976 Summer Olympics. Jenner eventually switched her name to Caitlyn in 1991. Kardashian got stepbrothers Burton "Burt," Brandon, and Brody, as well as stepsister Casey and half-sisters Kendall and Kylie, due to their marriage.

Kristen Mary Houghton, more commonly known as Kris Jenner, was born in San Diego, California, on October 5, 1962. When their parents separated, she and her younger sister moved to Claremont, California, with her mother, where she studied at Longfellow Elementary School. She then developed a cancerous bone tumor a year after her parent's divorce. Luckily, it did not spread and was successfully removed. She graduated from Claremont High School and did not pursue college; instead, she trained to be a flight attendant. Kris was 17 and in a relationship with Cesar Sanudo when she met Robert Kardashian. Kris and Cesar broke up after being caught having an affair with Robert. On July 8, 1978, Kris married Robert and had four children: Kim, Kourtney, Khloe, and Rob. Their family gained national recognition in the 1990s when Robert became the lawyer of O.J. Simpson. Robert and Kris divorced in 1991 after Kris cheated on Robert. Robert Kardashian died of esophageal cancer in 2013. She remarried in 1991 to Bruce (Caitlyn) Jenner, whom she met on a blind date, and became his manager. She and Bruce had Kendall and Kylie, then got divorced in 2014.

Their known family reality show, Keeping Up With The Kardashians, started when Kris met with Ryan Seacrest and pitched the idea in 2007. She branded herself as a "momager" for being the manager of her children. She is now a media personality, producer, manager, and business-woman. She also co-founded California Community Church with Pastor Brad in 2012. She is currently with her longtime lover, Corey Gamble, a music producer who started dating in 2014. We all know Kris Jenner does have pretty amazing genes. The 'Momager,' who has six children from two marriages, raises children and hedge fund managers. Now her kids are having babies at an alarming rate, and we're finding it difficult to keep track of the Kardashian children.

Robert George Kardashian was a lawyer and entrepreneur from the United States. Throughout O. J. Simpson's 1995 murder case, he rose to fame as Simpson's acquaintance and public defender. With his first wife, Kris Kardashian, he had four children: Kourtney, Kim, Khloé, and Rob, who star in the popular television show Keeping

Up with the Kardashians and its sequels. He was among the co-founders of Radio & Records, a marketing firm that he and his colleagues purchased for substantial revenue in 1979. Also, Kardashian was the first to introduce making songs in theaters during films. He went on to turn the entrepreneurial mindset, forming Movie Tunes. He was the company's President and CEO and subsequently bought in Juice Inc., a frozen yogurt company. In July 2003, Kardashian was hospitalized with esophageal cancer. Two months later, on September 30, 2003, he passed away at 59.

Kris Jenner, their mom, is of Dutch, English, Irish, and Scottish descent, and their father is an Armenian American of the third generation. Khloe was born in a nationally renowned family who got even more prominent after releasing a TV series revolving around their life.

4

GROWING UP WITH KOURTNEY KARDASHIAN

Kourtney's relationship with her family has many ups and downs, and they all had a fair share of drama. Their lives have been an open book to the media with the reality show they're starring in. Although they had many arguments, they always found a way to fix them and stronger bonds. Kourtney's stepfather came out as a transwoman in 2015 and wrote a book about his life, which caused a debacle in Caitlyn's relationship with the Kardashians. Kourtney grew up in the spotlight alongside her siblings, and they have a powerful bond. Kourtney even recognizes her half-sister, Kylie, and Kendall Jenner, as one of her support systems. Her siblings have an intense relationship with the model. One couple of weeks after her separation from Robert Kardashian, Jenner married her second husband, Bruce Jenner. Bruce Jenner is now Khloe's stepdad. Khloe's step-siblings are Brody Jenner, Burt Jenner, Brandon Jenner, and Cassandra Marino. Bruce

Jenner's children with Linda Thompson and Chrystie Jenner.

She went to Marymount High School in Los Angeles, a Roman Catholic all-girls institution.

After Kourtney finished her high school years, she went to Dallas, Texas, to pursue Southern Methodist University for two years. Kardashian then moved to Tucson, Arizona, during which she earned a college degree in Theatre Arts, with her taking a minor in Spanish from the University of Arizona. Nicole Richie and Luke Walt were among her colleagues.

KOURTNEY KARDASHIAN'S PERSONAL
RELATIONSHIPS

From 2006 to 2015, Kardashian was in an on-again, off-again relationship with Scott Disick. They interacted at a house party in Mexico hosted by a friend, Joe Francis. Kardashian and Disick have three children: Mason Dash Disick, Penelope Scotland Disick, and Reign Aston Disick. Keeping Up With the Kardashians and its countless spin-offs have featured Kardashian and Disick's on-again, off-again affair. The program has also documented Kardashian's childbearing and childbirth among all three children. The couple temporarily relocated to Miami with their son and Kim Kardashian's sister in early 2010. Kardashian thought Disick would have an alcoholism issue at the moment. But upon undergoing counseling on a routine basis and temporarily abstaining from alcohol, Disick and Kardashian reunited and resumed their connection in mid-2010.

Although Disick started asking Kardashian about the

wedding, she replied, "If matters are so great now...why should we choose to consider changing that?" and he decided not to propose.

Between 2017 to 2018, Kardashian has been in an on-again, off-again romance with model Younes Bendjima. Kardashian and her children were christened at the Etchmi-adzin Cathedral in Vagharshapat, Armenia, inside an Armenian Apostolic service in October 2019. Gayane, her Armenian name, was given to her during the service.

6

THE RISE OF KOURTNEY KARDASHIAN

Kardashian first gained popularity on television programs in 2005 with the show Filthy Rich: Cattle Drive, wherein she raised money for a good cause. Kim Kardashian, Superstar, a sex tape created by her sister Kim and former boyfriend Ray J in 2003, was unveiled in February 2007, mainly contributing to her rise to fame. Earlier that same year, Kardashian was cast in the reality tv show Keeping Up with the Kardashians alongside her mom Kris, stepfather Bruce, brother and sister Kim, Khloé, and Rob half-sisters Kendall and Kylie. The show was a massive success for E!, the station that broadcasts it, and it spawned numerous spin-offs, which include Kourtney and Khloé Take Miami, Khloé, and Lamar, and Kourtney and Kim Take New York. Kardashian and her mom launched Smooch, a kids clothing retailer in Los Angeles and New York City that carries the Crib Rock Couture brand. This program was a huge hit, and Kourtney Kardashian gained much attention and popularity. The

American model made a starring appearance in the ABC soap opera "One Life to Live," portraying attorney Kassandra Kavanagh. The television star's second series, "Kourtney and Khloé Take the Hamptons," premiered in 2014.

They earn $75,000 for each post on Social media, Facebook, and Twitter for waist-slimming jeans, cosmetic goods, and Coca-Cola. Kardashian began an every-week four-hour session show with Miami Top 40 Mainstream exposure WHYI on May 29, 2009, co-hosted by Terrence J. of 106 & Park. Kourtney Kardashian is a successful business owner to become a model and a television show host. Kris and her mother launched the 'Smooch' clothing and accessories retailer. There are many clothing store locations in New York City and Los Angeles. Kourtney also co-owns and runs a clothing store called DASH. By her sisters, the American beauty started a fashion brand for the Bebe company in 2010. Kardashian and her sisters launched a sunless tanner named "Kardashian Glamour Tan" in that same year. Not only that! The Kardashian sisters have also started a jewelry line for the business Virgins, Angels, and Saints. Kourtney Kardashian is a spokesperson for the 'Quick Trim' body fat vitamin. She and her sisters also embody a skin care products business. Dr. Ron DiSalvo created this line, dubbed "perfect skin." The Kardashian siblings also wrote a book called 'Kardashian Konfidential,' published in 2010. Kourtney Kardashian appeared in two parts of the sitcom "I Am Cait" in 2015. For that year, she even had a starring part in the film "Dash Dolls.

SIGNIFICANT CAREER MILESTONES

The show was a massive success for E!, the station that broadcasts it, and it spawned numerous spin-offs, which include Kourtney and Khloé Take Miami, Khloé, and Lamar, and Kourtney and Kim Take New York. Kardashian and her mom launched Smooch, a kids clothing retailer in Los Angeles and New York City that carries the Crib Rock Couture brand. This program was a huge hit, and Kourtney Kardashian gained much attention and popularity. The American model made a starring appearance in the ABC soap opera "One Life to Live," portraying attorney Kassandra Kavanagh. The television star's second series, "Kourtney and Khloé Take the Hamptons," premiered in 2014. Kourtney, however, has identified herself as that of the family's very ecologically minded individual. She attended a congressional conference on financial reform for the fashion sector in April 2018. She received an open invite from the charitable Environmental Working

Group, gaining recognition using her "fame" to bring attention to the subject.

Kourtney Kardashian is a successful business owner to
become a model and a television show host. Kris and her
mother launched the 'Smooch' clothing and accessories
retailer. There are many clothing store locations in New
York City and Los Angeles. Kourtney also co-owns and runs
a clothing store called DASH. By her sisters, the American
beauty started a fashion brand for the Bebe company in
2010. Kardashian and her sisters launched a sunless tanner
named "Kardashian Glamour Tan" in that same year. Not
only that! The Kardashian sisters have also started a jewelry
line for the business Virgins, Angels, and Saints. Kourtney
Kardashian is a spokesperson for the 'Quick Trim' body fat
vitamin. She and her sisters also embody a skin care products business. Dr. Ron DiSalvo created this line, dubbed
"perfect skin." The Kardashian siblings also wrote a book
called 'Kardashian Konfidential,' published in 2010.
Courtney Kardashian appeared in two parts of the sitcom "I
Am Cait" in 2015. She even had a starring part in the film
"Dash Dolls."

KOURTNEY'S FRIENDS AND FOES

The lengthiest on-again, off-again dispute on Keeping Up With the Kardashians came to an end in previous episodes, when Kourtney and Kim Kardashian — sisters, business associates, and sworn enemies — stepped into some physical battle. Another thing went through a segment of KUWTK in 2019, viewers witnessed Kardashian and her younger sister Kendall Jenner argue over peers. Jenner is 16 years Jenner's junior, and the model has started accusing her older sister of becoming "rude" with Jenner's peers. While Jenner's issue was clearly that she had been attempting too hard to satisfy her peers, several people seem to find it "weird" that Kardashian spends too much time with young people these days. Of course, several fans believe there is nothing inappropriate with Kardashian fitting alongside her age. Many individuals, for example, are supportive of socializing with individuals who are significantly older or younger than them, particularly in professional settings.

.   .   .

AFTER HER FAMILY'S documentary series, Keeping Up With the Kardashians, debuted in 2007, Kourtney Kardashian has become a media personality. Given the amount of publicity Kardashian, including her family, gets daily, it's unsurprising that they're criticized on various issues. Fans are perplexed by Kardashian's tendency to socialize with people far younger than herself these days. Kardashian, a 41-year-old mother of three, manages to be around individuals even a decade younger. Some supporters say that was "odd" and aren't hesitant to voice their thoughts on Kardashian's connections. Addison Rae, a 19-year-old social media influencer who rose to fame last year on TikTok, appears to be one of Kardashian's latest acquaintances. Once Rae featured in a workout program with Kardashian, the two were first connected. The two of them started appearing interacting more often on Instagram and TikTok.

FUN FACTS ABOUT KOURTNEY

Along with her unique taste and the way she dresses, Kourtney Kardashian is among the Kardashian sisters everyone constantly talks about. The Kardashian-Jenners have been saying that becoming a billionaire does not require a bachelor's degree. Just one of the Kardashian daughters does have a college diploma: Kourtney Kardashian received a bachelor's degree in theater from the University of Arizona. At the same time, Rob accompanied in Kourtney's footsteps and attended the University of Southern California because none of the sisters did. Kourtney started working as a film production secretary in college. She told Us Weekly in 2010 that the job required her to shout and scream "cut" and "roll" daily. Indeed not as abundant as her current lifestyle. Kourtney Kardashian has a long list of broadcast credits upon making an appearance in her family's tv program for 12 years, and therefore she didn't seem to stop there. She made a guest appearance in 2011 on a scene of ABC's popular tv drama One Life to Live, in which she got to play Kassandra Kavanaugh, an attorney.

10

HOW THE WORLD SEES KOURTNEY KARDASHIAN

Kardashian first gained popularity on television programs in 2005 with the show Filthy Rich: Cattle Drive, wherein she raised money for a good cause. Kim Kardashian is mainly contributing to her rise to fame. Earlier that same year, Kardashian was cast in the reality tv show Keeping Up with the Kardashians alongside her mom Kris, stepfather Bruce, brother and sister Kim, Khloé, and Rob half-sisters Kendall and Kylie. The show was a massive success for E!, the station that broadcasts it, and it spawned numerous spin-offs, which include Kourtney and Khloé Take Miami, Khloé, and Lamar, and Kourtney and Kim Take New York. Kardashian and her mom launched Smooch, a kids clothing retailer in Los Angeles and New York City that carries the Crib Rock Couture brand. This program was a huge hit, and Kourtney Kardashian gained much attention and popularity.

Kourtney Kardashian's endorsements made her earn $75,000 for each post on Social media, Facebook, and

Twitter for waist-slimming jeans, cosmetic goods, and Coca-Cola. Kourtney Kardashian claims to be endorsing her brother-in-law Kanye West's run for the presidency when she appeared for her 102 million followers on Instagram wearing a "Vote Kanye" cap. In an October 15 Instagram account, Kourtney Kardashian, the famous Television family's oldest daughter, endorsed her brother-in-law Kanye West's election candidacy. The Kardashians, who have no boundary for promoting companies on their social media accounts, were taken aback by the advertised slot in people's timelines. Kourtney Kardashian has been the sibling who has the fewest advertised posts on social media. And it's a fraction of what her sisters have. But, on the other hand, she has a lot fewer fans than they do. After all, it's just 45 million people. Fit Tea and Fit Coffee claims to be a natural tea or coffee that comprises a potent perfect blend that has been around for decades for its beneficial effects worldwide. Fit Tea is a company in which both Khloe and Kylie have collaborated, so it's no wonder that Kourtney does as well. Manuka Doctor creates beauty treatment solutions that are naturally based, clinically improved, and 100 percent bee safe. And I believe you can all conclude that Kourtney is an excellent match for this business, as she follows a consistently safe and organic diet. It's no wonder that Kourtney is featured over the front cover.

Through her preferred Calvin Klein undergarments, Kourtney exhibits with her fiance. The tag line alone gives little to the intuition, except the hashtags indicating that the content is endorsed. It's almost caption-less. CK has been a media platform's influencer-friendly brand, with the hashtag #MyCalvins circulating for weeks. As a result, it's no wonder that perhaps the Kardashians, as advertiser celebrities, were approached for a brand collaboration. Diff

Eyewear is an eyewear company that takes satisfaction in helping the community; with every pair of glasses purchased, the company donates prescription glasses and vision welfare services to those in need. Kourtney, who comes from one of the most influential individuals in the world of style, collaborated with FashionNova on a range of endorsed Instagram stories. Through the brand's feud with Kourtney's sister, Kim, Kourtney has not declined to form long-term relationships with FashionNova.

KARDASHIAN and her family are baptized at the Etchmiadzin Cathedral in Vagharshapat, Armenia, in an Armenian Apostolic service in October 2019. She was given the Armenian surname Gayane, however, during ceremonies.

KARDASHIAN HAS BECOME a supporter of the Armenian Genocide Monument in Yerevan, Armenia, and has toured Tsitsernakaberd, a remembrance to the deceased. Kardashian have spoken in favor of the Republic of Artsakh and Armenians during October 2020, criticizing Azerbaijan's participation and the 2020 Nagorno-Karabakh war. She appeared on the ArmeniaFund philanthropy telethon on October 10, 2020, and encouraged audiences to consider donating donations to rebuild those involved in the current conflict.

KOURTNEY KARDASHIAN IS confident of her appearance and tries to resist the trolls as much as she can. The television personality, who is 40 years old, opened up about maintaining her mental wellbeing from online harassment.

Although she acknowledges that there is still a lot of bitterness on the internet, she also points out that there is a lot of optimism. Supporters have noted that at least one Kardashian appears to have her priorities straight regarding physical aspects. Kourtney Kardashian is sending out big self-acceptance positive energy, and the media is loving it.

REFERENCES:

Https://peoplepill.com/people/kourtney-kardashian/
Kourtney Kardashian - Bio, Facts, Family & Love Life of Model & Reality Star (thefamouspeople.com)

Kourtney is the Most Body-Positive Kardashian, And People Can't Get Enough (cheatsheet.com)

A Full Breakdown Of All The Kardashian And Jenner Grandchildren (elle.com)

The Kardashians: 10 surprising facts about the children of Kim, Kourtney, Kylie, and Khloe | HELLO! (hellomagazine.com)

Kourtney Kardashian - Reality Television Star - Biography

33 Crazy Facts You Never Knew About the Kardashians | Best Life (bestlifeonline.com)

Kourtney Kardashian appeared to endorse Kanye West's presidential run, advertising his campaign merch on her Instagram story | Business Insider India

Brand Guide To Kourtney Kardashian Instagram Posts (hollywoodbranded.com)

Fans Think It's 'Weird' That Kourtney Kardashian Has So Many Young Friends (cheatsheet.com)

Kourtney Kardashian Says She's 'Proud' of Her Body After Gaining 'A Few Pounds Over This Quarantine' | Entertainment Tonight (etonline.com)

Kourtney Kardashian Quits 'KUWTK' After Fight With Kim (vulture.com)

Photo Credits

 ourtney Kardashian for a GQ phostohoot in 2018

21 February 2019

https://commons.wikimedia.org/wiki/
File:Kourtney_Kardashian_for_GQ.png
Kourtney Kardashian attending Maxim's 10th Annual Hot 100 Celebration, Santa Monica, CA on May 13, 2009 - Photo by Glenn Francis of www.PacificProDigtial.com

13 May 2009

https://commons.wikimedia.org/wiki/File:
Kourtney_Kardashian_2_2009.jpg
Kourtney Kardashian for a GQ phostohoot in 2018

February 2019

Britt Bellamy / CC BY (https://creativecommons.org/li-
censes/by/3.0)
https://commons.wikimedia.org/wiki/File:
Kourtney_Kardashian_for_GQ_-_4.png
Kourtney Kardashian for a GQ phostohoot in 2018

21 February 2019

Britt Bellamy / CC BY (https://creativecommons.org/li-
censes/by/3.0)
https://commons.wikimedia.org/wiki/File:
Kourtney_Kardashian_for_GQ_-_2.png